An introduction by John A. Lent

WAS IT WORTH IT?

A Collection of International Cartoons about Columbus and His Trip to America

edited by
Michael Ricci
and
Joseph George Szabo

WittyWorld Publications
North Wales, PA

WittyWorld Publications'
international cartoon magazine
reaches over one hundred
countries worldwide. The works
presented in this book were
selected from a wide array of
international submissions.

Special thanks go to
Robert Byers, for his generosity
made this book possible.

BOOK DESIGN: JOSEPH STARLIGHT
ADMINISTRATIVE
ASSISTANT: BRIAN HARLING
PRINTED IN HONG KONG.

ACKNOWLEDGEMENT IS MADE OF GLORIA DEAK'S ARTICLE
IN THE SEPTEMBER 1991 AMERICAN HERITAGE, WHICH WAS A
MAIN SOURCE FOR PARTS OF THE INTRODUCTION.

ISBN: 0-9631600-0-1

COVER ART: MARCO DE ANGELIS
BACK COVER: LJUBOMIR SOPKA

WittyWorld Publications
P.O. Box 1458, North Wales, Pennsylvania 19454
United States of America

Introduction

The story of Christopher Columbus' "discovery" of the Americas is a complicated one--replete with myths, inaccuracies, and controversies. It has varied from the romantic bare-bones version of Columbus as a brave and humane explorer, foisted upon children in their earliest school experiences, to the revisionist accounts of Columbus as the slave trader and inept administrator under whose rule, cruelties occurred. The latter gained some favor during the approach of the five-hundredth anniversary of the feat.

Of course, Columbus' "discovery" of the New World is a myth in itself. The native Americans had arrived thousands of years before, having navigated their way in makeshift rafts from somewhere in the mid-Pacific, as Thor Heyerdahl contended, or having walked across a land bridge that once connected Asia with North America. In fact, Columbus was not even the first European to touch American soil, credit for that going to St. Brendan and the Irish in the seventh century and the Vikings in the eleventh century. Myth also has it that Columbus stood alone in his belief that the earth was round. Not so. All educated people knew differently, as did sailors from experience. University geography classes taught the concept that the earth was a sphere. The real controversy of Columbus' time was the size of the earth, most scientists underestimating it by as much as two-thirds of its circumference.

Myth also surrounds where Columbus thought he was when he landed. Did he think he was in India since he did name the inhabitants "Indians"? Not necessarily. Columbus had no idea where he was, although he had hoped to reach the Indies, a term applied more broadly to eastern Asia, including Cathay, Japan, Burma, Indonesia, India, and Moluccas. A belief common among many people today is that Columbus "discovered" the United States. (Cartoonists in this volume take liberty with where he actually landed.) His first landing was on San Salvador, a Bahamian island (not the Central American city). He apparently never stepped foot on the mainland of North America in any of his trips.

Other inaccuracies have abounded. One concerned his nationality, confused because so many nations claimed him as one of their own, but also because of his numerous domiciles. Columbus was born in Genoa of Italian parents, contrary to claims that he was of Spanish, Portuguese, Catalan, or Jewish ancestry. After leaving Italy, he lived in both Portugal and Spain, where beginning

PRINT DEPARTMENT, NEW YORK PUBLIC LIBRARY

The artist tried to get a panoramic view of the expedition in this woodblock print from a 1493 publication of Columbus' letter announcing his discovery. King Ferdinand is at left, naked native Americans in a tropical setting at right, Columbus' three ships at center foreground, and a European city at bottom.

6

before 1484, he petitioned these countries' monarchs to support his "Enterprise of the Indies" scheme. Ironically, although King John II of Portugal was the first to turn down his petition (King Ferdinand and Queen Isabella of Spain did also before granting permission in 1492), it was to him Columbus first reported his achievement. He found himself in this predicament when, on his return from America, he had to seek permission for his battered ship to enter a Portuguese seaport.

Astonishing as that report to King John II must have been (in light of the fact Columbus was accompanied by some of the native Americans he had brought back), it paled in comparison to the more sensationalistic account given

Naked inhabitants of the New World figured in a few of the early depictions of Columbus' discovery. In fact, this is one of the earliest known portrayals of the native Americans, published as part of Columbus' letter. The native Americans are seen fleeing into the trees as two explorers are about to step ashore. The Santa Maria is in the foreground.

by Amerigo Vespucci, who explored South America after Columbus' initial journeys. He reported in lurid detail of cannibalism and sexual promiscuity among native Americans, which guaranteed him instant popularity (people's interests do not change much, do they?). In fact, because Vespucci was a better public relations man than Columbus, the new world was named after him by Geographer Martin Waldseemuller, when he charted the discoveries in 1507 and considered Vespucci's accomplishments more significant.

Columbus made four voyages to America. During his first trip in 1492, he explored a number of islands of the Caribbean and established a settlement, La Navidad, on the large island he called Hispaniola. He left 39 men behind to search for gold and to further develop the colony. However, when he returned to the islands in November 1493, he found none had survived. They had fallen victim to internal squabbles brought on by their greed for gold and local women (men's lusts do not change much, do they?). Columbus' second voyage was his grandest. Queen Isabella and King Ferdinand of Spain provided him a fleet of 17 vessels and a crew of 1,300 men for an adventure that was to last two and one-half years. The monarchs' goals were to expand Christianity, convert the natives, and seek gold. Columbus had another motive to find the Asian mainland which he thought was in the vicinity of his explorations. Instead, he "discovered" many more islands, including Cuba and Dominican Republic, set up three additional settlements in the New World (only one of which, Santo Domingo, survived), and began his brutalization of the native Americans. The Spaniards forced the people they called Indians to search for gold and exterminated those who refused. Five hundred were shipped to Spain as slaves, but only 300 survived the journey.

His third trip was longer in coming, for the glory Columbus had known was being passed on to other explorers such as Vasco da Gama and Giovanni Caboto. In 1498, he set sail again, this time with eight ships, ever in quest of a westward passage to the Asian mainland. He explored Venezuela and Trinidad before being arrested in Hispaniola by representatives of the Spanish crown. The charge was mismanagement of colonial affairs. He and his brothers Bartolomeo and Diego were returned to Spain in 1500 in chains. Upon clearance by a Spanish court, Columbus strove to pull together a fourth expedition. After a long wait, he was granted permission to sail in 1502, but with the conditions that he be accompanied by a comptroller to watch over any riches he found and that he be under the jurisdiction of a newly-appointed governor who had replaced him.

Some artists of the day rendered their ideas about the exploits of Columbus. In fact, Columbus' letter describing his first voyage, published in Basel in 1493, contained two woodcuts. One showed La Navidad, the first settlement; the other, about a dozen naked native Americans fleeing two of the crew members making their way to shore in a boat launched from the Santa Maria. Both are carica-

RARE BOOKS AND MANUSCRIPTS DIVISION, NEW YORK PUBLIC LIBRARY.

A third print from the Basel publication of Columbus' 1493 letter exaggerates La Navidad, the first European colony. The buildings were not built that solidly nor did they have tile roofs.

turized portrayals. A German woodcut of 1505 showed native Americans in a variety of activities, including roasting and eating parts of a human, breast-feeding a child, and making love. Nearly a century later, Flemish artist Theodore de Bry did many prints recording Columbus' activities, including some that did not happen, such as Ferdinand and Isabella's farewell visit to Columbus at the docks.

The cartoonists whose work make up this book look at Columbus' achievements in a multitude of planes. Some transpose the explorer in space and time. Thus, there are cartoons of Columbus wearing Mickey Mouse ears or dreaming of what he might find in America (Marilyn Monroe). Two cartoons remind us that without Columbus' "discovery," there might not have been landings on the moon. A modern day Japanese discovery and takeover of the United States figure in at least two cartoons.

A few themes are particularly popular. Many cartoonists deal with cultural exchange or cultural invasion. Some depict paraphernalia of modernity already on the beaches when Columbus arrived, things such as Coca-Cola, lounge chairs, tropical

TOPKAPU SARAY MUSEUM, ISTANBUL.

Rumors spread fast and far about the New World and its inhabitants. This 1513 drawing that was part of a map prepared by Turkish Admiral Pirl Reis showed native Americans as bodyless.

drinks, surf boards, beach umbrellas, bingo tickets, timesharing, CNN, football and baseball teams ("Redskins" and "Indians," of course), money exchanges, duty free shops, "discounts for discoverers," Disneyland, McDonald's hamburgers, and Toshiba radios. In a few cases, the cartoons show native Americans readying themselves for the tourism that Columbus represented to them, i.e., the toll gate, hotels, and duty free shops. In addition to tourism, Columbus is shown exporting pizza (home delivery, no less), but forgetting his American Express card.

Modern day advertising is spoofed in a cartoon showing Columbus' ship plastered with decals much as sports equipment and locations are today.

continent populated by European-Americans; adding to a list of Spaniard promises, those of "Alcoholism, herpes, and lousy housing conditions," and daydreaming about cultural/educational rewards of Spanish colonization, while the Spaniard is thinking of rape, plunder, and slaughter.

Other cartoons find the native American worn down, drinking and homeless; loading up his ark as the first drops of the end-of-the-world rains (Columbus' arrival) began, and wondering what harm a "few boatloads of white refugees" can do. Also in this latter category are cartoons showing the native American drawing "Yankee Go Home" graffiti on the stones, exclaiming "There goes the neighborhood," or wondering "What they want."

Allusions to Western civilization's impact upon environment and health can be found here too. Columbus gets a glimpse of what the future holds for America (pollution, crime, noise, overcrowding). In one cartoon Columbus receives directions: "America? Easy! Go past three oil spills,...." Overcrowded metropolises figure in some works; one shows the lushness of the America to which Columbus sails, counterbalanced with the crowded cities today, from which populations fly, seeking isolated, lush areas elsewhere.

A couple of cartoons portray the adverse effects of imported alcohol upon the native Americans and of exported tobacco upon the Europeans. Strangely, no cartoon is included that alludes to the possibility that Columbus' crew took syphilis back to the Old Continent.

The earlier-mentioned myths surrounding Columbus' voyages are dealt with by these cartoonists. One has a youngster asking, "What year was it that the native Americans discovered Columbus?". Others portray the Spaniards deciding to erect a founding-

The native American in his canoe was drawn from life in the Caribbean Islands by Fernandez de Oviedo in the early 16th century.

HENRY E. HUNTINGTON LIBRARY.

The disastrous consequences of Columbus' landing are plentifully evident. The exploitation, enslavement, and eventual extermination of the native American appear in numerous works. There is a depiction of the native American screaming for help as he is isolated on a tiny atoll offshore a of-the-nation memorial on the spot where a couple of native Americans stand and Vikings claiming Columbus' arrival was doing a "number on our new world time share." Columbus' confusion about where he was shows up in a cartoon that has a Spaniard mocking the explorer, saying that if they go further, they will find Turkey (in this case, the bird).

Works are featured that emphasize positive results of Columbus' adventure, such as the one that has people of different nationalities jumping into a ditch in the shape of the United States on one side, and all climbing out as supermen on the other. Another shows Columbus being carried by six native Americans, each wearing the headgear of a future United States icon--Liberty, astronaut, Mickey Mouse, etc. The implication is that without Columbus, all of these would have been impossible.

The compilers of this book have done an excellent job soliciting and choosing cartoons by artists from 38 countries. The works included provide perspective on the facts, myths, and consequences of Christopher Columbus' achievement. However, from my reading of the cartoons here, the answer to the thematic question, "Was it Worth It?" is a resounding "no!". But then, one would not expect otherwise; cartoonists normally prick our consciences with the blemishes--the pimples and warts--of society, and in this case, of history. That is why we need them so much.

John A. Lent

Both the native Americans and Spaniards have been portrayed as practicing cruel deeds. Here, in a German woodcut from about 1505, one native American is seen munching on a human arm, while the rest of the torso roasts over fire.

Equally lurid is this depiction of Spanish savagery to native Americans in the Caribbean region. It is from a 1598 book by Bartolome de Las Casas, considered a friend of the native Americans. Hands are amputated, eyes are gouged out, and native Americans are fed to animals.

MORRIE TURNER
United States of America

HOW CAN WE HELP YOU, ROCKY?
WHAT YEAR WAS IT THAT THE NATIVE AMERICANS DISCOVERED COLUMBUS?
MORRIE
6-3

JAVIER COVO T.
Colombia

PEDRO PENIZZOTTO
Argentina

"SOME DAY SON, ALL THIS WILL BE YOURS..."

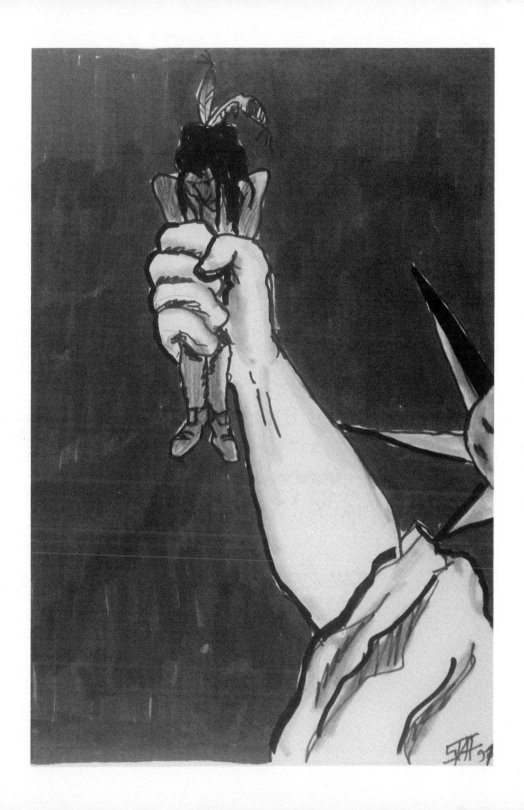

GUSTAAF LAMBRECHT
Belgium

MIKE TURNER
United States of America

"THERE GOES THE NEIGHBOURHOOD".

off

FRANTISEK JURACKA
Czech and Slovak Republic

VLADIMIR BALCAR
Czech and Slovak Republic

MOHSEN NAJAFI
Iran

BILL GRIFFITH
United States of America

"ZIPPY DISCOVERS AMERICA"

MIROSLAV MRAZEK
Czech and Slovak Republic

OLDRICH DVORAK
Czech and Slovak Republic

GOURGIOTIS SPIROS
Greece

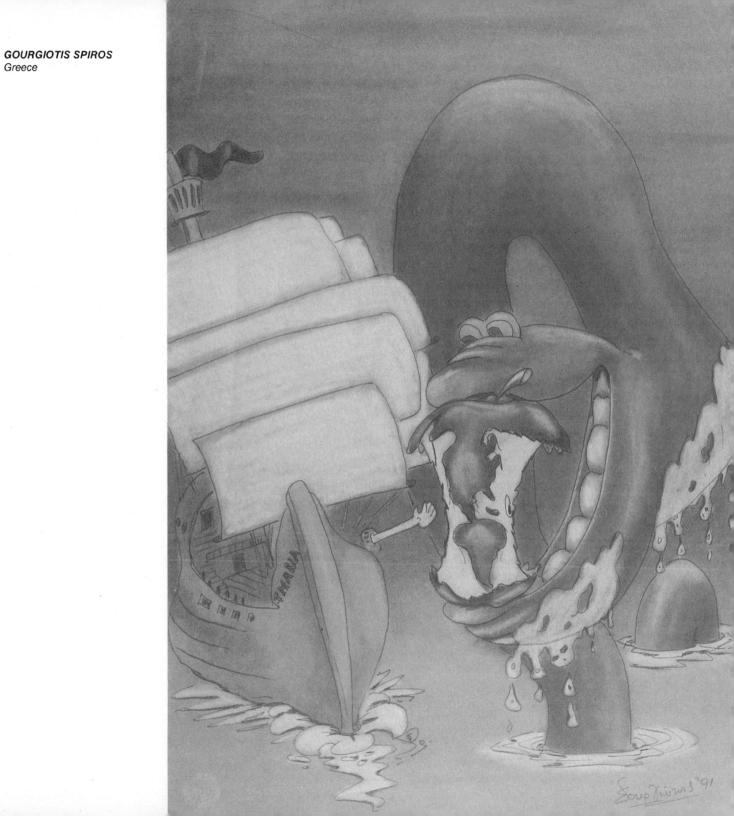

FRANK PAUER
United States of America

THE 500th ANNIVERSARY OF THE DISCOVERY OF AMERICA

THE 500 th ANNIVERSARY OF THE DISCOVERY OF AMERICA

TOMAS KOZYRA
Australia

CHAN LOWE
United States of America

"WANT TO BUY SOME BINGO TICKETS, PALEFACE?"

ROMAN LANG
Germany

THERESA McCRACKEN
United States of America

WHAT DO YOU MEAN WE LEFT HOME
WITHOUT AN AMERICAN EXPRESS CARD?

"IT COULD BE MORE OF A HEALTH HAZARD IF YOU *DON'T* SMOKE IT!"

TIM ERNST
Japan

JAVIER COVO T.
Colombia

DAVID ANDERSON
South Africa

SERGIO IRACHETA
Mexico

LAJOS BALOGH
Hungary

JIM BERRY
United States of America

BUTCH JEGERE
United States of America

PETE WILLIAMS
England

"NATIONAL GEOGRAPHIC AREN'T GOING TO LIKE THIS..."

DENG COY MIEL
Philippines

JEAN-LOÏC BELHOMME
France

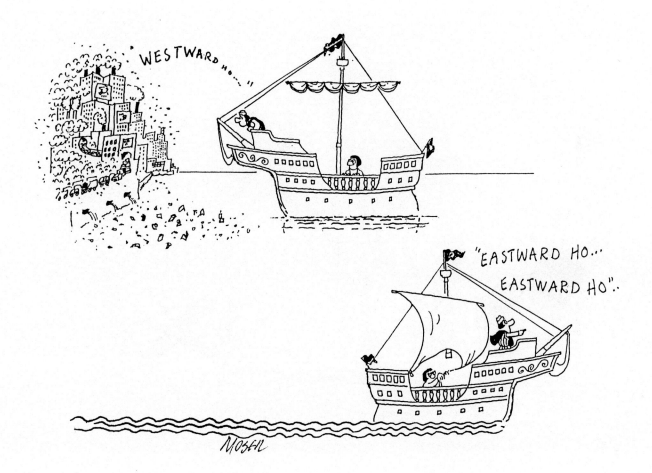

HANS MOSER
Switzerland

GENNADY JAKSHIN
Ukraine

ALEXANDER SHABANOV
Russia

IVAN HARAMIJA
Croatia

JOE HELLER
United States of America

AREND VAN DAM
Netherlands

POPPE HERMANN
Belgium

ANATOLIJ GILEV
Russia

GARY KELL
United States of America

MARCO DE ANGELIS
Italy

LOUIS POSTRUZIN
Australia

ANATOLIJ GILEV
Russia

BOB DARROCH
New Zealand

JOHN. R. CASSADY
United States of America

"NOW DO YOU BELIEVE IN U.F.O.'S?"

GEORGE BREISACHER
United States of America

SCOTT JOHNSON
United States of America

"GREAT! LET'S SEE IF WE CAN UNLOAD MANHATTAN ON THEM."

JAVIER COVO T.
Colombia

ANDRZEJ CZYCZYTO
Poland

BUSINESS OR PLEASURE?

FRANZ FÜCHSEL
Denmark

WHO'S NEXT?

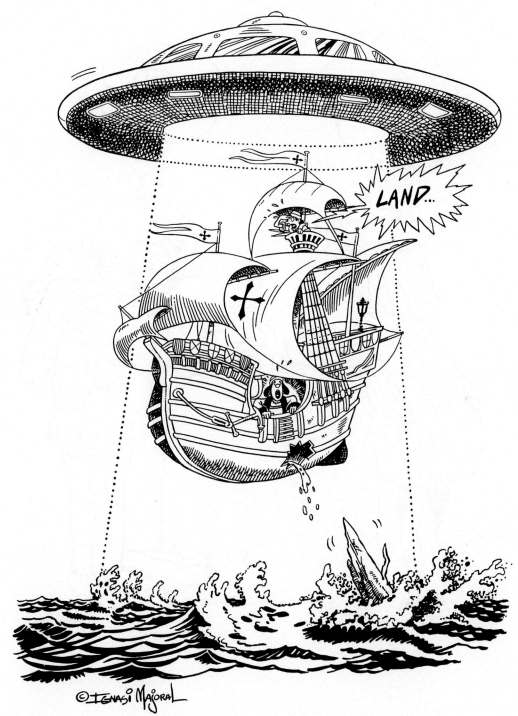

76

GHEORGHE CHIRIAC
Romania

LEONID STOROZHUK
Ukraine

JEAN-LOÏC BELHOMME
France

ANATOLIJ GILEV
Russia

PETE WILLIAMS
England

LISTEN UP — THERE'S A GUY CALLED COLUMBUS TRYING TO DO A NUMBER ON OUR NEW WORLD TIMESHARE . .

SERGEI TUNIN
Russia

82

ULISES CULEBRO BAHENA
Spain

"America? Easy!... Go past three oil spills... Hang a left at the floating medical waste... And it'll be the big toxic burial site straight ahead..."

84

NOAM NADAV
Israel

GÁBOR PINTÉR
Hungary

SERGEY KHASABOV
Russia

DAVE COVERLY
United States of America

"FASCINATING REPORT, MR. COLUMBUS, TRULY FASCINATING...
BUT SURELY YOU DISCOVERED **OTHER** THINGS IN THE
NEW WORLD AS WELL,..."

AHMET ERKANLI
Turkey

JEAN-LOÏC BELHOMME
France

ANTONIO MOREIRA ANTUNES
Portugal

MARK F. LYNCH
Australia

"IT WILL BE ALRIGHT, YOUR MAJESTY - I HAVE A GUIDE!"

WILFRIED GEBHARD
Germany

"NOW YOU TELL ME YOU'RE STRICT VEGETARIANS!"

ELZBIETA SIDOROWICZ
Poland

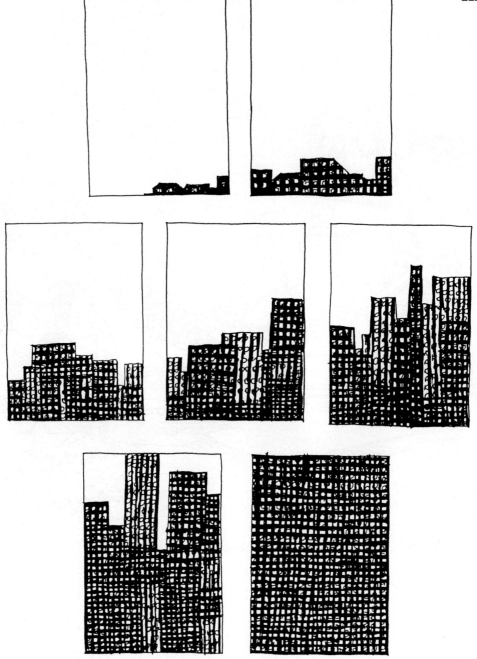

WAS IT WORTH IT?

EDD ULUSCHAK
Canada

LÁSZLÓ DLUHOPOLSZKY
Hungary

GODERIS LUDO
Belgium

HAVE YOU EVER BEEN OR ARE YOU A MEMBER OF A COMMUNIST PARTY, DO YOU WANT TO WORK HERE ??

WILLIAM GOODWIN
Australia

I DON'T BELIEVE IT PAOLO... NOW THE OLD BOY RECKONS
IF WE KEEP GOING WEST WE'LL FIND TURKEY!

JURAS VISOCKIS
Lithuania

Index

Argentina
Blumen-Calliera 73
Pedro Penizzotto 16

Armenia
Fljian & Samuelian 86

Australia
William Goodwin 106
Tomas Kozyra 28, 29
Mark F. Lynch 94
Louis Postruzin 63

Belgium
Beldho 56
Poppe Hermann 60
Gustaaf Lambrecht 17
Goderis Ludo 104, 107

Brazil
Erico O. Junqueira Ayres 45

Canada
Brian Gable 54
Lo Linkert 97
Vance Rodewalt 69
Geoffrey Smith 101
Edd Uluschak 102

Colombia
Javier Covo T. 14, 37, 70

Croatia
Ivan Haramija 57
Davor Trgovcevic 49

Czech and Slovak Republic
Vladimir Balcar 21
Oldrich Dvorak 24
Frantisek Juracka 19,20
Miroslav Mrazek 23

Denmark
Franz Füchsel 74

England
Alan de la Nougerede 95
Pete Williams 46, 80

Estonia
Heino Prunsvelt 15

France
Jean-Loïc Belhomme 48, 78, 92
Roger Mofrey 100

Germany
Wilfried Gebhard 96
Roman Lang 32

Greece
Gourgiotis Spiros 25

Hungary
Lajos Balogh 41
László Dluhopolszky 103
Gábor Pintér 87

Iran
Mohsen Najafi 22

Israel
Mik Jago 39
Noam Nadav 84

Italy
Marco De Angelis, cover, 63

Japan
Tim Ernst 36

Kazakhstan
Danilenko & Kadyrbaev 27

Lithuania
Juras Visockis 108

New Zealand
Bob Darroch 66

Mexico
Sergio Iracheta 40

Netherlands
Willy Lohmann 89
Arend Van Dam 59

Philippines
Deng Coy Miel 47

Poland
Andrzej Czyczyto 72
Piotr Kakiet 55
Elzbieta Sidorowic 98

Portugal
Antonio Moreira Antunes 93

Romania
Gheorghe Chiriac 76
Olas Doru-Ghiocel 99

Russia
Anatolij Gilev 61, 64, 79
Sergey Khasabov 88
Vladimir Nenashev 85
Alexander Shabanov 53
Sergei Tunin 81

Singapore
Ken Lou 71

South Africa
David Anderson 11, 38

Spain
Ulises Culebro Bahena 65, 82
Ignasi Majoral 75

Switzerland
Hans Moser 50, 51
Pfuschi 31

Turkey
Ahmet Erkanli 91

Ukraine
Leonid Storozhuk 77
Gennady Jakshin 52

United States of America
John Bell 109
Jim Berry 42,43
George Breisacher 67
John R. Cassady 67
Dave Coverly 90
Bill Griffith 22
Joe Heller 58
Butch Jegere 44
Scott Johnson 68
Gary Kell 62
Laser and Langer 105
Chan Lowe 30
Jimmy Margulies 83
Theresa McCracken 34
Frank Pauer 26
Dan Piraro 33
Frank Taylor 35
Morrie Turner 12, 13
Mike Turner 18

Yugoslavia
Ljubomir Sopka, back cover

Joseph George Szabo, an entrepreneur and accomplished cartoonist whose published works span five continents, is founder and editor-in-chief of *WittyWorld International Cartoon Magazine*. Szabo also initiated and co-organized the first Budapest International Cartoon Festival and is editor of a new book series titled "Best International Political Cartoons of the Year".

Michael Ricci has had a life-long interest in comic art and is currently working on several cartoon related publishing projects.

John A. Lent, Ph.D., managing editor of *WittyWorld International Cartoon Magazine,* is the author of approximately 40 books and hundreds of articles, many of which deal with comic art.